Text & Illustrations by Kenneth M. Jones

First Published 1977.

ISBN 0 85524 279 2

Distributed in the U.S.A. by
Squadron/Signal Publications Inc.,
3461 East Ten Mile Road,
Warren, Michigan 48091.

Printed in Great Britain by
Staples Printers Ltd.,
Trafalgar Road, Kettering,
Northamptonshire,
for the publishers, Almark Publishing Co. Ltd.
49 Malden Way, New Malden,
Surrey KT3 6EA, England.

No. 2 BRITISH
NORTH AFRICA

D0756871

By
Kenneth M. Jones

Almark Publishing Co. Ltd.,
London

INTRODUCTION

Although the campaign against the Italians in North Africa did not actually commence until war was officially declared against Italy on 10th June 1940, Britain had undertaken the task of building up a sizeable force in North Africa from the early thirties. This formation became entitled 'The Mobile Force' – which was euphemistically dubbed 'The Immobile Farce' – and was formed on the 17th of September, 1938 from elements of the Cairo Cavalry Brigade. This new formation had varied equipment and very few tanks; those on strength were mainly light tanks armed only with heavy and medium calibre machine guns, for which ammunition was in short supply.

Major-General P. C. S. Hobart was sent to Egypt to organise the proposed new formation, which he reshaped into a much stronger force by the latter end of 1939, when he was succeeded in command by Major-General O'Moore Creagh. The Mobile Division became the famous 7th Armoured Division on the 16th February 1940. Hobart had formed a force that could at least take to the battlefield. At the end of the same year the British attacked the Italians, defeating all in their path. Until the arrival of the advance elements of the German Afrika Korps, who were soon to form, with the Italians, Panzer Armee Afrika, the British had things much their own way. After the debacle in Greece, which had cost Wavell good men and badly needed material, the British were hard pushed to contain the attacking Axis force. If Wavell had sent what Churchill required him to over to Greece, matters would have been far worse than they were. The British experienced two consecutive failures during Operations 'Brevity and Battleaxe'; the latter left the Germans and Italians commanding Halfaya Pass, resulting in amongst other things Winston Churchill replacing General Wavell with General Auchinleck.

General Auchinleck launched an offensive which was codenamed Operation Crusader. He attacked the Axis on a 50-mile front with the combined strengths of XIII and XXX Corps, driving the German Italo Force back to El Agheila. General Auchinleck failed to follow through with this offensive and the British were soon to regret this descision in the battles that followed throughout the early part of 1942, now commonly known as the Gazala Battles. These actions ended with the surrender of the Allied Force at Tobruk on 21st June 1942. Tobruk had been Rommel's goal from the outset of the German presence in North Africa, though after its capture he was unable to press on with the attack due to a lack of equipment and supplies, although he had taken a considerable amount of useful war material at Tobruk. Even with this 'booty' there was not enough of the essentials to supply his highly mobile panzer columns.

The British withdrew to the more defensible 'line' at El Alamein. Two battles around Alamein were to follow. The first battle changed the overall situation only slightly; except once again Churchill replaced the British Commander, General Auchinleck with General Harold Alexander, and General Montgomery was made commander of The Eighth Army.

Montogomery soon had to face an attack launched by Rommel in August, this was the Battle of Alam Halfa. The Axis were stopped in their attempts to take the ridge at Alam Halfa and they pulled back to a defensive position stretching between the coast and the Qattara Depression. It was this defensive 'line' that the Eighth Army attacked on 23rd October 1942, driving forward on a broad front out of their Alamein position, the outcome of which is well known. Early the next month the Axis were in full retreat. The United States Army landed in North Africa and after initial setbacks and defeats against the battle-experienced Afrika Korps did much to bolster the Allied Force in Tunisia, through to the surrender of Axis Forces in North Africa in May 1943.

The British had maintained a presence in North Africa with a force of mainly light tanks and armoured cars, 'strengthened' with adhibited supplies of trucks and other soft skin equipment. When war became imminent the, then, latest marks of Cruiser Tanks were rushed to the war zone. These were the tanks that had fought with the B.E.F. in France, but were not really suited to desert operations. These vehicles were the A9's, A10's, A13's and A15's known in British nomenclature as 'Cruiser Tanks'. The Matilda was omni-present in the early campaigns, the British calling this an 'Infantry Tank', intended to support the infantry in the assault. It had thick armour, but was very slow; its armour was proof against contemporary German and Italian anti-tank guns, though the later 50mm and of course the 88mm gun could penetrate its armour. British tanks did not fare very well in desert conditions, mechanical breakdown was commonplace, and the narrow tracks bogged down very easily in soft sand. Deliveries of American tanks, the M3 Stuart Light Tank and the M3 Mediums, The Grant and Lee, later to be eclipsed by the M4 Sherman which arrived in the desert in time for the great Alamein offensive. These American tanks gave the Allies a larger dual purpose gun, the 75mm which could take on German armour at longer ranges than experienced previously with the standard British tank gun, the 2 pounder.

The British possessed good soft skin transport of both indigenous and Commonwealth manufacture, which served them well in the desert. The Afrika Korps, always short of equipment, put British trucks to good use, whenever possible, often as self-propelled gun mounts, bedecking them with large markings to clearly indicate the current owners nationality. British armoured cars, especially the later Humbers and A.E.C.'s were good in the reconnaissance role, though transmission and engine life was short in the arduous conditions they encountered. With an extensive supply back-up, the British were never as short of equipment as their foes. The Royal Navy ruled the Mediterranean sealanes and the Commonwealth Airforces had command of the air. With the large supple depots and rest areas to the rear, in Egypt, the British soldier had far more apparent advantages than his German or Italian opponents had.

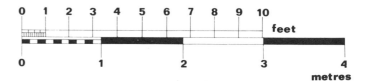

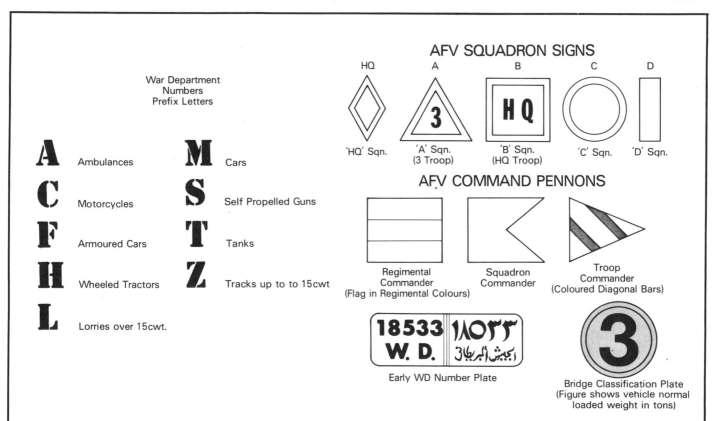

War Department Numbers Prefix Letters

A Ambulances

C Motorcycles

F Armoured Cars

H Wheeled Tractors

L Lorries over 15cwt.

M Cars

S Self Propelled Guns

T Tanks

Z Tracks up to to 15cwt

AFV SQUADRON SIGNS

'HQ' Sqn.

'A' Sqn. (3 Troop)

'B' Sqn. (HQ Troop)

'C' Sqn.

'D' Sqn.

AFV COMMAND PENNONS

Regimental Commander (Flag in Regimental Colours)

Squadron Commander

Troop Commander (Coloured Diagonal Bars)

Early WD Number Plate

Bridge Classification Plate (Figure shows vehicle normal loaded weight in tons)

CAMOUFLAGE APPLICATION

The British vehicles that were in North Africa at the outbreak of war were finished – usually – in an overall desert sand coloured finish. The Royal Air Force, who kept a force of armoured cars, to protect and police its airfield perimeters, finished these in a similar fashion, though the markings that R.A.F. vehicles carried were slightly different. Tanks, armoured cars and lorries were finished in a light sand colour, much lighter than the German sand paint (RAL 800) which faded to an even lighter shade from the ravages of use and exposure to the desert enviroment. Prior to the outbreak of war all British military vehicles carried civilian type number plates fore and aft; these were bolted onto a vertical surface, or as near to the vertical as possible on tanks and other armoured vehicles.

After commencement of hostilities, all vehicles that were shipped out to the Middle East were finished in dark earth with or without a disruptive darker pattern painted on. On arrival these vehicles were taken into base workshops and modified for desert operations, which included a coat of sand coloured paint overall. Thin metal dustguards were fitted over the running gear, the function of which was not to reduce the dust set up by a moving vehicle (this is bordering on the impossible to effect in practice) but to deflect the dust and sand thrown up by the tracks down and away from the engine compartment and air intakes. This becomes apparent if photographs are scrutinised of the early model Crusaders that served in the desert. Base workshops fitted the majority of this early batch with rear dust guards (similar to the pattern found on the A13 Cruiser Tanks) to keep sand away from the carburettor intakes on the rear trackguards. Whether these were entirely successful in operation it open to doubt as the mechanical failure rate amongst British tanks was high. In addition to sandguards, extra stowage racks and stringers were bolted or welded onto vehicles to enable the crew to stow their personal equipment; interior space on vehicles was at a premium, and extra fuel, water and other material had to be carried, attached to the outhsides of the vehicle.

An interesting finish was applied to British armoured vehicles during the early part of the North African Campaign. It was a triple-colour combination of dark earth, or dark grey, dull blue and desert sand. The overall appearance of the vehicle was broken up by these colours, but their intensities soon faded with wear and the attentions of the elements which deposited an overall layer of dust – not always the best camouflage incidentally – which seemed to mock the obvious careful attention lavished onto these vehicles when the finish was applied. The triple combination did not last long and soon gave way to an overall sand finish or to the later dual scheme of sand and charcoal. The three colour finish was painted on with straight sharp-edged demarcation lines which usually tapered all the colours to a point at the rear of the vehicle roughly down its centre line. Generally a plain sand finish was more commonly encountered, though as always there was a lot of individual 'efforts' in evidence. Vehicles were painted in disruptive patterns of sand and khaki, or with broad charcoal patches, the majority being brush painted, leaving hard demarcation lines. Some units painted on the khaki disruptive pattern and edged it with a darker paint; perhaps black. As always (it even happens today in a peacetime army) crews were left to get on with their own camouflage schemes.

With most painted finishes a lot of variation in shades of colour will be found, just as there were a lot of variations to the official standard recommended finish. Some interesting special-purpose finishes were evident such as shading out the three centre roadwheels with black paint on the Crusader Tank and fitting it with a detachable hesian tilt to disguise its appearance in an attempt to make it appear as a heavy lorry to distant enemy observers. This guise was carried out on different types of tank, and was not peculiar to the Crusader. Cement was occasionally used by British tank crews. It was mixed up and spread in random patches over the vehicle, followed by handfuls of sand scattered over the wet cement. The cement was then allowed to dry into the natural camouflage colour effected by the sand application. This was only really suitable if the colour of the terrain did not alter much. As anyone who has been in a desert area knows the terrain changes quite considerably; even over a short distance both geography and colours can change.

When compared with their German and Italian counterparts the British and Commonwealth Forces had a wide selection of markings – often very colourful ones! – that could be displayed on their vehicles. Two schools of thought were present here; some applied only the bare minimum although alternatively photographs show us just about every imaginable marking displayed. More often than not soldiers like a bit of 'swank' and try to be one up on the next vehicle in the platoon, or for instance a commanding officer would like to see his formation as 'the' formation and as a direct result some rule-bending would take place, often bordering on the esoteric, subject to his personal fads or whims. These variations make research on the subject very difficult – but interesting nevertheless – and very confusing at times.

British vehicles, armoured and soft skin types would usually display a War Department Number, which was painted onto a clearly visible flat surface, or as was found on some lorries following the curve on the side of the bonnet lid. This number, painted in either white or black (it was often any colour to hand) was prefixed by a letter which designated the type. The numerical element belonged to consecutive numbered blocks allocated to batches of vehicles. Painted on WD numbers superseded the civil-type registration plates that were fitted to military vehicles. Early in the desert campaign, the 'Red-White-Red' recognition marking painted onto vehicles was very common. Although its usage declined later in the war, some of the Crusader Tanks that belonged to the 17th/21st Lancers, 26th Armoured Brigade, 6th Armoured Division, had small versions of this motif painted onto their hull sides, and the front and rear plates, during the closing days of the campaign in Tunisia. This marking was also carried on vehicles in Italy, the Sherman Tanks of The Royal Scots Greys being only one example. One cannot help thinking what an ideal aiming-point this bright-coloured swatch made to an enemy gunner. British tanks carried pennons on their aerial masts that indicated the command vehicles within each formation, and also as signal flags for passing instructions to vehicles in the formation. The hoist position of these pennons varied on the aerial masts in accordance with orders of the day.

Arm-of-service markings were coloured squares painted onto vehicles whenever possible, and were displayed fore and aft. They identified the operating service by the colour of the square and subordinated the unit by a number painted onto it. The numbers were changed for security reasons and should have been changed – but not always – with the order of battle within a formation. Some examples are shown in the colour pages. Arm-of-service markings is a vast subject by itself and can only be briefly touched upon here. The arm-of-service marking was usually fixed or painted directly onto the right side of the vehicle, on the hull front or the dustguard. Opposite this sign was either emblazoned the divisional or brigade sign. Quite

often higher formation signs were displayed, and these with the arm-of-service marking, taken in conjunction with any other signs displayed completely subordinated the vehicle to its unit, but only at the time of application. Regrouping and reforming of both new and old units in the desert war did little to help anyone researching the markings.

Squadron markings were displayed in the officially recommended or any other available colours by tanks, armoured cars and some soft skin vehicles that were included within armoured formations. These marks took the form of triangles, squares and circles, each indicating to which squadron a tank belonged and they were usually painted onto the turret sides; the platoon number was painted inside this device. Photographs of the period show the squadron signs to be of varying sizes, with little standardisation regarding sizes or application. Personal names could be used in conjunction with squadron signs – names beginning with 'A' for A Squadron vehicles, 'B' for B Squadron and so on. This practice was not always rigidly applied and all sorts of names were found to be painted onto vehicles by their crews, from wives' and girlfriends' names, to football teams' and placenames. Some were very carefully executed and appear to have been done by signwriters in uniform, or artistically-minded soldiers. Generally speaking rear echelon equipment offered the more lavish efforts.

Other markings in evidence were the yellow bridging circles with a black number painted inside it to denote the bridging class of the vehicle. Bridging class plates were displayed on all types of vehicle. Wheeled vehicles often had their tyre-pressures painted above each wheel, on the mudguards, in white or black. These were the officially stated pressures for the tyres in use on the vehicle, taken from the the vehicle handbook.

Markings – of the British Army in North Africa alone – is a vast subject. In this book we have only really scratched the surface, and have had to make a broad analysis in what could be included. It is hoped that what has been included will act as a primer on the subject to anyone having interests in the British and Commonwealth Forces that fought in North Africa during World War Two.

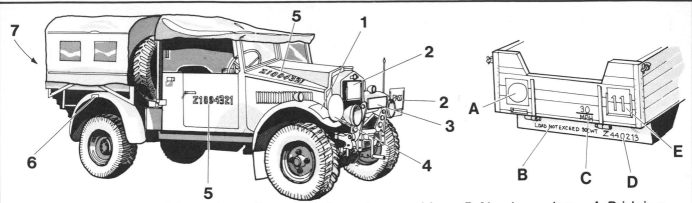

1. Formation sign. 2. Locations for arm-of-service marking. 3. Number plate. 4. Bridging classification. 5. WD number. 6. Tyre pressure lbs per square inch. 7. Markings repeated on rear.

A. Formation sign. B. Loading restriction. C. Speed restriction. D. WD number. E. Arm-of-service plate (Reverse was khaki with "PASS" in white)

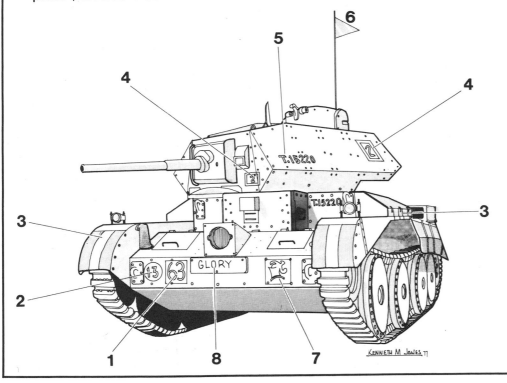

KENNETH M JONES 77

1. Arm-of-service marking. 2. Bridging classification. 3. Red, white, red recognition stripes. 4. Squadron marking. 5. WD number (repeated on hull front and rear). 6. Pennon indicating command tanks and for visual signals. 7. Divisional marking. 8. Vehicle 'nickname'.

6

ABOVE: At Tobruk two Marmon Herrington Armoured Cars lie beyond this knocked-out Cruiser Mark IV A of C Squadron 5th Royal Tank Regiment, 2nd Armoured Division. The unit number, 63, has been roughly painted onto a green square under the headlamp and the 2nd Armoured Division's badge appears on the left hull front. Clearly visible on the turret front plate is C Squadrons tactical marking. The number 10 which appears within the circle is the troop number. (IWM).

RIGHT: German troops on the Tobruk perimeter examine a British Cruiser Mark IV A (A13 MKII) formally of 5th Royal Tank Regiment, the junior regiment of 3rd Armoured Brigade, 2nd Armoured Division. The arm-of-service marking, 63, was painted onto a green square as the 3rd Armoured Brigade were the junior brigade. The 2nd Armoured Division badge, a plumed knight's helmet in white on a red square is barely visible on the front plate. B Squadrons tactical marking is just visible under the turret revolver port. (IWM).

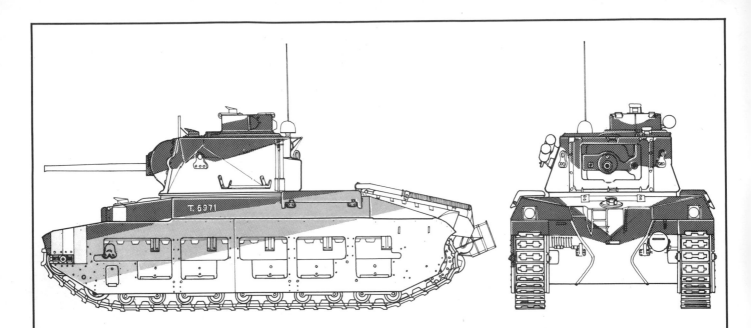

INFANTRY TANK MARK IIA* MATILDA III (A12)

CREW	4
ARMAMENT	1 × 2 Pdr (40mm) OQF Gun 1 × 7.92mm Besa Machine Gun 1 × .303in. (7.7mm) Bren Light Machine Gun AA on Lakeman Mounting. 2 × 4 in. Smoke Dischargers
ENGINE	Twin LEYLAND 6 cylinder water cooled diesels.
BATTLE WEIGHT	26.5 tons
MAXIMUM SPEED	15 mph (24 kph)
ROAD RANGE	160 miles

ABOVE: This Vickers Mark VI B light tank has been disabled and abandoned by its crew. It bears evidence of having been finished in the diagonal striped sand, blue and dark earth camouflage. The whole turret rear plate has been painted red-white-red, and the personal name 'Churchill' neatly painted on the turret side. The WD number, partly obscured, is T22636. (IWM).

LEFT: Bold charcoal stripes have been painted onto this sand finished Valentine, photographed near El Alamein. The camouflage stripes have been painted onto the upper surfaces, as the pattern can be seen on the open flap of the turret hatch. Note the Bren Machine Gun mounted in a 'crutch' on the turret roof for AA use. The crewman in front of the vehicle is assembling his 'stove' for brewing tea, making good use of a halt for refreshments. The 'stove' consisted of a tin filled with sand saturated with petrol. When lit this concoction burned long enough to boil water for teamaking. (IWM).

Photographed on the 10th of April 1942, this Indian Wheeled Carrier MK II on patrol bears some interesting clear markings. The vehicle has a personal name Dhar V, there being a IV and VI in the unit. The yellow bridging circle bears the number six. Opposite is the Indian arm-of-service marking, a white figure 9 on a red square. Above this is the motif of the 10th Indian Division. The Indian pattern number plate, white digits on black with a WD-type arrow was common to all Indian vehicles. This carrier is sprayed an overall sand. It is armed with a Boys Anti-Tank Rifle in the front plate and a Vickers Berthier Machine Gun for AA use. (IWM).

A 25 pounder field gun in action on the 1st of June 1942 at Knightsbridge. Both gun and limber have been camouflaged with darker paint, probably dark earth, in tiny patches over the sand finish. This is clearly shown on the open limber door. This pattern is not common on British equipment in North Africa, broad stripes and large patches being more frequently seen. (IWM).

General Auchinleck in his Ford Heavy Utility at El Daba on the 2nd July 1942. Supplied to commanders, these 'station wagons' were useful roomy vehicles, being both comfortable and fast. General Auchinleck's car has been modified to take roof hatches over the cab, and a roof rack has been fitted. Three petrol cans have been mounted over the rear wheel arches. The bracket half way along the bonnet behind the union flag is a sun compass mounting. The camel badge of GHQ Middle East is painted onto a metal plate which slides into the bracket on the mudguard. The reverse of this plate would be khaki with the word 'pass' painted on in white. The windscreen has been smeared with mud to reduce reflections.

An oversize 1st Armoured Division badge has been painted onto the side of this Bantam 40 BRC. This well-known photograph (the man in the passenger seat is HRH The Duke of Gloucester) shows the size of badge more commonly seen on tanks. Note the symmetry of this oval-shaped badge indicating the use of a template in its application. The Bantam is sand overall with a darker colour, possibly a light earth, forming a wavy disruptive pattern. The diamond probably represents the HQ squadron symbol, as found on tanks. (IWM).

This Daimler 'Dingo' bears the markings of the 7th Armoured Division, the red Jerboa being clearly visible. This particular Dingo belongs to 5th Royal Tanks, bearing the unit number 67 stencilled in white onto a green square as 5 RTR were in 22nd Armoured Brigade at this time who were the junior brigade of the 7th Armoured Division. On the original print the arm-of-service mark appears to have been overpainted in a lighter shade (green) because 5 RTR were formally in 4th Armoured Brigade and would have used red markings, the 4th being the Senior Brigade. Note that the sergeant Bren Gunner has 5 RTR strips on his epaulettes. The vehicle number F19377 has been stencilled on. (IWM).

MORRIS ARMOURED RECONNAISSANCE CAR (C9)

SCOUT CAR MK IB

1st Armoured Division

2nd Armoured Division

6th Armoured Division

8th Armoured Division

8th Army

1st Army

10th Armoured Division
(variant)

10th Armoured Division

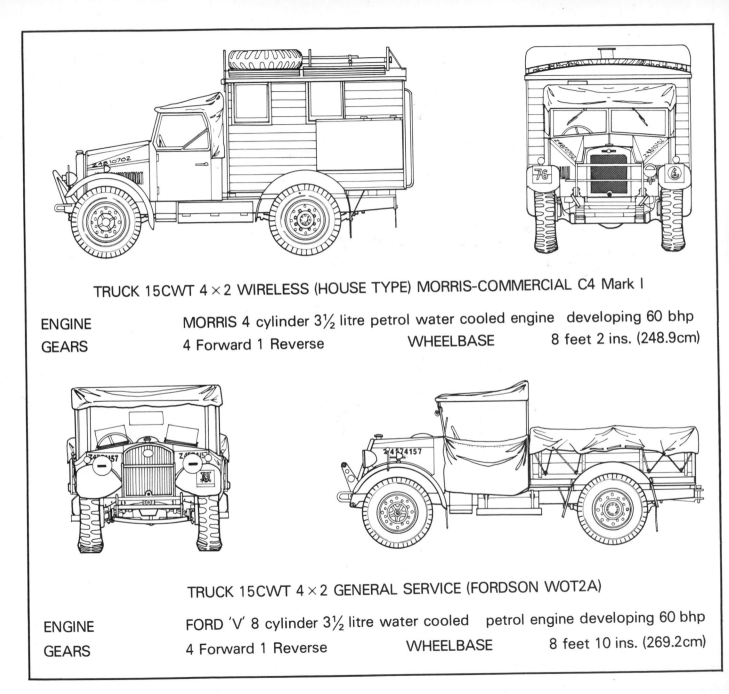

TRUCK 15CWT 4 × 2 WIRELESS (HOUSE TYPE) MORRIS-COMMERCIAL C4 Mark I

ENGINE   MORRIS 4 cylinder 3½ litre petrol water cooled engine developing 60 bhp

GEARS   4 Forward 1 Reverse   WHEELBASE   8 feet 2 ins. (248.9cm)

TRUCK 15CWT 4 × 2 GENERAL SERVICE (FORDSON WOT2A)

ENGINE   FORD 'V' 8 cylinder 3½ litre water cooled   petrol engine developing 60 bhp

GEARS   4 Forward 1 Reverse   WHEELBASE   8 feet 10 ins. (269.2cm)

TOP LEFT: A Royal Engineer's tank destruction team in a 'Dingo' observing their next 'victim'. These teams would drive onto battlefields and blow up enemy tanks to deny their recovery. This 'Dingo' carries the red desert rat or Jerboa on a white disc within a red square. The number 33 is in white on a blue square identifying this vehicle as belonging to Army Troops Company, Royal Engineers. The vehicle is in sand overall with light charcoal or khaki strips. Note the neatly stencilled WD number (IWM).

LEFT: The co-driver of a Fordson 13 cwt truck takes a 'sight' with his compass. The truck sports a two-tone camouflage which has been brush painted. Over the bonnet lid the vehicle number has been neatly stencilled on. This truck belongs to the 7th Armoured Division though its unit is not known. The diamond on the cab door is the HQ symbol as used by armoured units. The tyre pressure, 25lbs per square inch has been painted onto the mudguard. (IWM).

TOP RIGHT: Using the turret of a Marmon Herrington Armoured Car for his pulpit, an army padre conducts a church parade for 8th Army personnel. The markings on the car – unfortunately – have received the attentions of the censor, even the WD number has suffered. The overall three-tone finish is evident on this well-weathered vehicle. In addition to its Boys Anti-Tank Rifle this Marmon Herrington has a German MG34 fitted into the turret. (IWM).

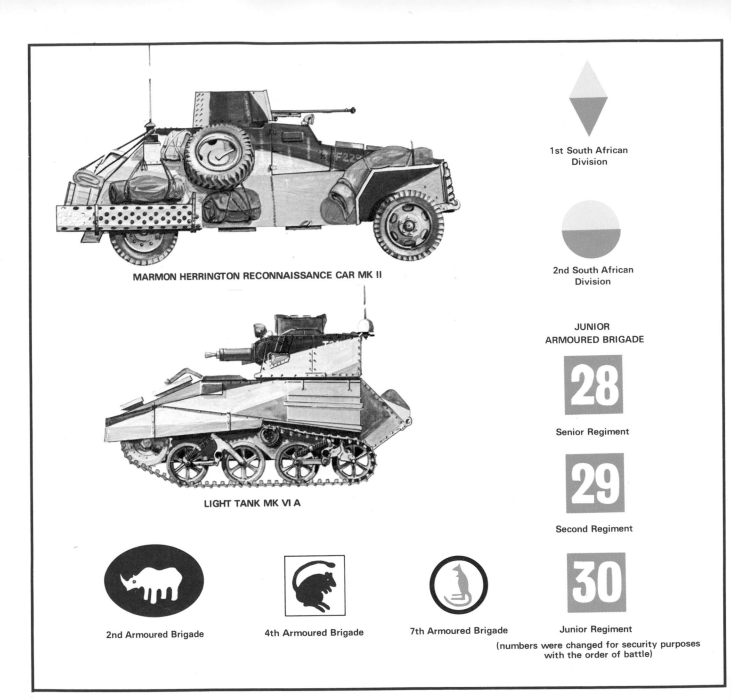

MARMON HERRINGTON RECONNAISSANCE CAR MK II

LIGHT TANK MK VI A

1st South African Division

2nd South African Division

JUNIOR ARMOURED BRIGADE

28

Senior Regiment

29

Second Regiment

30

Junior Regiment

(numbers were changed for security purposes with the order of battle)

2nd Armoured Brigade

4th Armoured Brigade

7th Armoured Brigade

SENIOR ARMOURED BRIGADE

Senior Regiment

Second Regiment

Junior Regiment

7th Armoured Division (early version)

7th Armoured Division (later version)

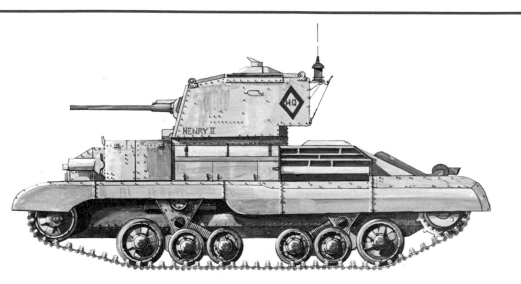

CRUISER TANK MK I (A9)

8th Armoured Brigade

9th Armoured Brigade

16th Armoured Brigade

MORRIS LIGHT RECONNAISSANCE CAR MK I

22nd Armoured Brigade

23rd Armoured Brigade

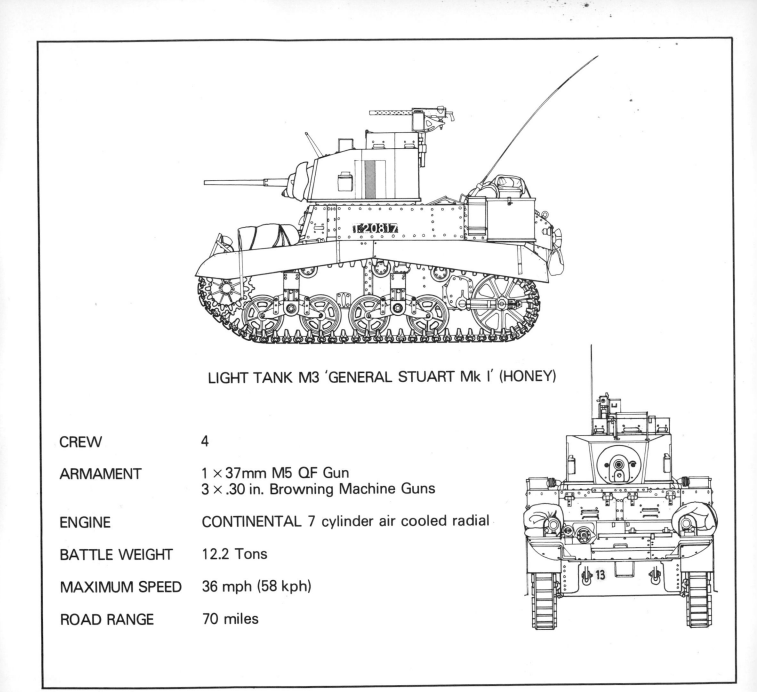

LIGHT TANK M3 'GENERAL STUART Mk I' (HONEY)

CREW	4
ARMAMENT	1 × 37mm M5 QF Gun 3 × .30 in. Browning Machine Guns
ENGINE	CONTINENTAL 7 cylinder air cooled radial
BATTLE WEIGHT	12.2 Tons
MAXIMUM SPEED	36 mph (58 kph)
ROAD RANGE	70 miles

LEFT: Taken during April 1942 this photograph shows General Rommel and his staff examining a captured M3 Light Tank supplied to the British from the United States of America. The photograph is interesting in that it shows the 'A' Squadron on the turret with HQ inside, indicating that the vehicle was from the headquarters troop within 'A' squadron. This 'Honey' has been finished in sand with a darker disruptive pattern sprayed on, evident on the original print. Compare the tank's finish with the overall grey on General Rommel's Kfz 15 car. (IWM).

RIGHT: HRH The Duke of Gloucester observing a shoot from an M3 Grant. The last three letters of the name 'Allenby' can be seen on the side of the 75mm gun sponson. This name was painted in white, as was the WD number onto the original olive drab finish and masked off when a thin coat of sand paint was applied, leaving the drab background showing through. (IWM).

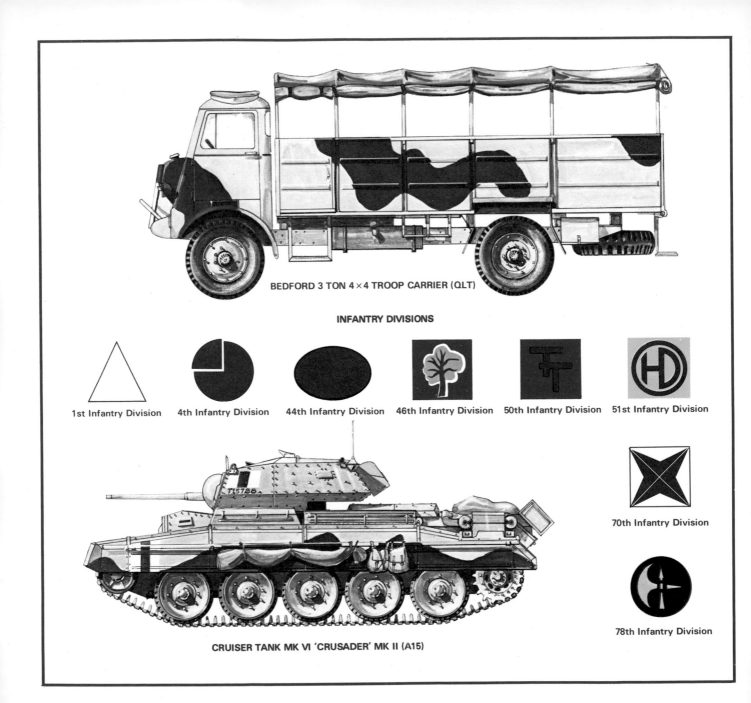

BEDFORD 3 TON 4×4 TROOP CARRIER (QLT)

INFANTRY DIVISIONS

1st Infantry Division

4th Infantry Division

44th Infantry Division

46th Infantry Division

50th Infantry Division

51st Infantry Division

70th Infantry Division

78th Infantry Division

CRUISER TANK MK VI 'CRUSADER' MK II (A15)

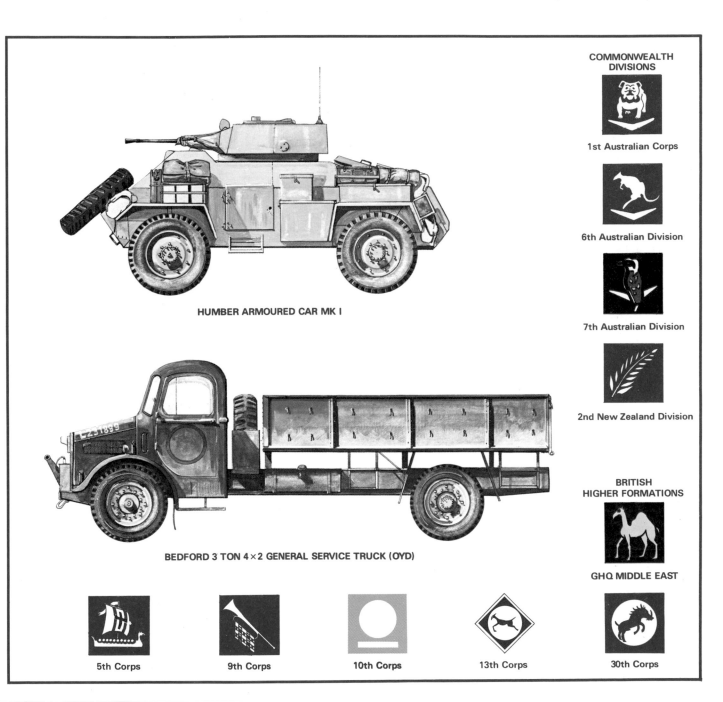

HUMBER ARMOURED CAR MK I

BEDFORD 3 TON 4×2 GENERAL SERVICE TRUCK (OYD)

COMMONWEALTH DIVISIONS

1st Australian Corps

6th Australian Division

7th Australian Division

2nd New Zealand Division

BRITISH HIGHER FORMATIONS

GHQ MIDDLE EAST

5th Corps

9th Corps

10th Corps

13th Corps

30th Corps

LEFT: The BBC War Correspondents operated from this Fordson WOT 8 30 cwt truck which has been modified into a recording caravan, enabling the correspondents to broadcast back reports on battles during the campaign. The vehicle is newly painted with neatly stencilled WD numbers on its doors and the bridge classification number on the disc which appears to have been oversprayed with the rest of the vehicle. A combined unit and corps badge has been painted onto the left-hand side of the vehicle front, consisting of the GHQ Middle East Badge, a gold or yellow camel on a black background and the unit number on the diagonally divided red and green arm of service mark of the RASC. The white bar under this signifies this vehicle was subordinated to Army Troops. (IWM).

BELOW: An AEC Matador Medium Artillery Tractor used for winching trucks up an incline bears the tiger's head insignia of the 1st Armoured Brigade Group over the unit number 38, painted onto a metal plate and affixed to the cab front. The tractor has been oversprayed sand as is clearly indicated by the darker surround to the WD numbers on the cab doors which were apparently masked off when spraying. (IWM).

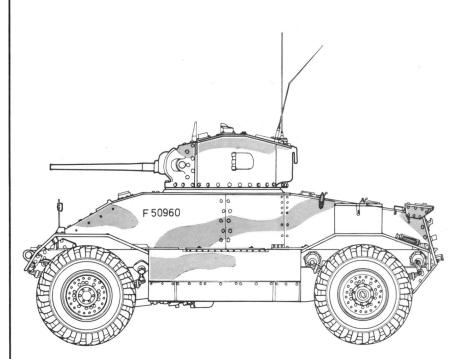
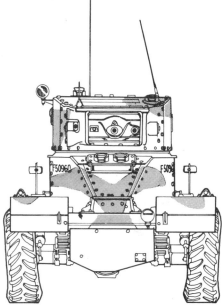

ARMOURED CAR AEC MK I

CREW	3
ARMAMENT	1 × 2 Pdr (40mm) OQF Gun 1 × 7.92mm Besa Machine Gun mounted co-axially 1 × .303 in. (7.7mm) Bren AA on Lakeman Mount
ENGINE	AEC 6 cylinder water cooled diesel
BATTLE WEIGHT	11 tons
MAXIMUM SPEED	35 mph (56 kph)

ARM OF SERVICE MARKINGS
(numbers were changed for security purposes with the order of battle)

99

Headquarters

76

Royal Artillery

84

Royal Army Service Corps

33

Royal Engineers

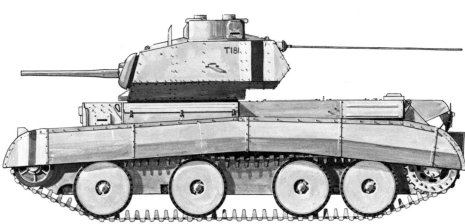

CRUISER TANK MK IV A (A13 Mk II)

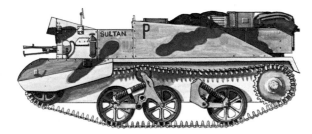

UNIVERSAL CARRIER

Vehicle Recognition Marking

4th Indian Division

5th Indian Division

10th Indian Division

3rd Indian Motor Brigade

31st Indian Armoured Division

General Alexander inspects Polish tank crews parading in front of their captured German Panzer III's which have been immaculately resprayed in British sand paint, anj given new markings. This photograph was taken on September 12th 1942 at The Middle East School of Artillery, Elmaza, near Cairo. These PzKw III's are in first class condition, replete with spare road wheels and tracks and have been given red, white, red recognition signs on the turret sides, continued down the hull sides. They have been given a consecutive monomic numbering system on the turret sides. Although it could be safely said that these tanks would not be, or were not used in action by the allies, their appearance is very interesting to modelling enthusiasts, especially those who may be looking for a totally different finish for their Panzer III's. (IWM).

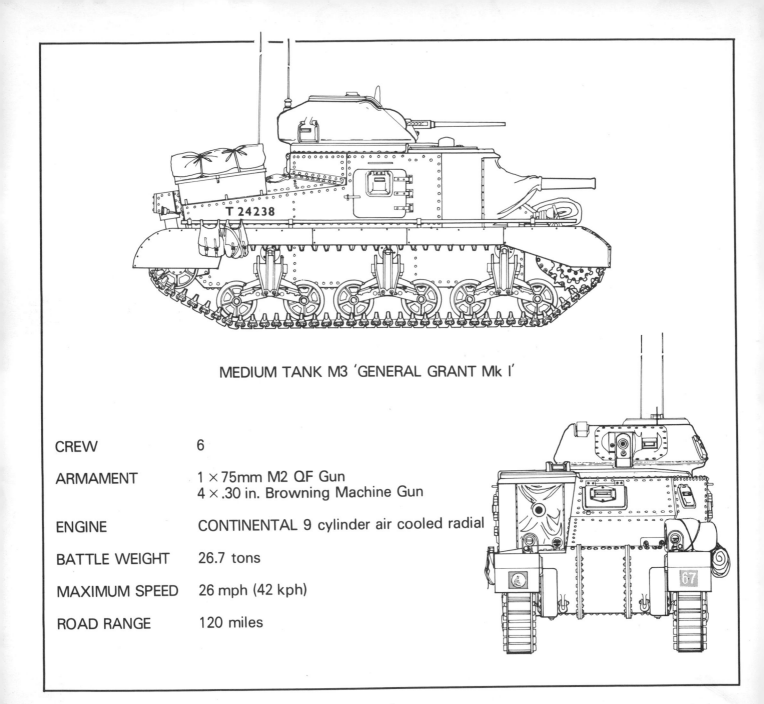

MEDIUM TANK M3 'GENERAL GRANT Mk I'

CREW	6
ARMAMENT	1 × 75mm M2 QF Gun 4 × .30 in. Browning Machine Gun
ENGINE	CONTINENTAL 9 cylinder air cooled radial
BATTLE WEIGHT	26.7 tons
MAXIMUM SPEED	26 mph (42 kph)
ROAD RANGE	120 miles

A. B: The crew of this M3 Grant have painted a personal name onto the turret side just in front of the squadron marking. The newly-painted name shows how much the rest of the tank's overall sand finish has faded with the attention of the elements. The personal name appears to have been done in a bright colour, probably red, and outlined in black. Personal names were popular with the tank crews and ranged from the one shown here to quite professional-looking attempts. The WD number is visible on this vehicle. It has been applied with a stencil, the webs of which are visible on the numerals. Points worthy of note are the 'common' form of stowage for the personal kit, the canvas cover for the 75mm gun mantlet, and the Browning Machine Gun mounted for AA defence with a spool for the ammunition supply. The inside of the access door is painted off-white, though interior surfaces of M3's were not always painted white. (IWM).

C: At the time this photograph was taken this M3 Grant belonged to the 5th Royal Tank Regiment, 4th Armoured Brigade, 7th Armoured Division. It mounts half of the metal and canvas framework that some tanks were fitted with to disguise them as heavy lorries. It was referred to – for security purposes – as a 'sunshade'. The markings carried are the 7th Armoured Divisions 'Jerboa' in red on a white disc within a red square on the left-hand trackguard. The right trackguard has an arm-of-service and divisional sign combined into one marking. The unit number, 86, was painted white on the square which was red, the

4th Armoured Brigade being the senior brigade in the division at this time. (IWM).

D: In this 'posed' photograph a tank gunner of the Warwickshire Yeomanry lectures his comrades on the 75mm gun, using a round to illustrate his points. His M3 Grant in the background carries a two-tone camouflage with darker demarcation lines. The colours are probably sand and khaki-brown with charcoal outlines. No other markings are visible on the original photograph of this vehicle. This colour scheme was common on M3's as photographic evidence shows though a plain overall sand was more usual, with or without any markings. Units did not always find time to paint on identification marks, though the tactical squadron markings were applied whenever possible as these immediately identified the tank to its squadron in the battle formation. The Warwickshire Yeomanry were in 9th Armoured Brigade which served as an independant brigade within the 2nd New Zealand Division. (IWM).

BELOW: Sherman III's (M4A2) of C Squadron, The Queens Bays, 2nd Armoured Brigade, 1st Armoured Division move through Gabes Gap in April 1943. These Shermans are sand with charcoal stripes sprayed on. The lead and third tanks show combined formation and arm-of-service signs, depicting the 'charging rhino' of 1st Armoured Division and the number 40 indicating the senior regiment. The turret side has been marked with a circle indicating 'C' Squadron and for The Queens Bays – who were senior regiment – this should be red. (IWM).

During the latter part of the North African Campaign the British received these American 105mm Howitzer Motor Carriage's, which they named 'Priest'. This dust covered example, crewed by members of the 11th Royal Horse Artillery, belonged to the 1st Armoured Division, the badge of which can be seen on the right front dust guard; on the left dust guard is the red over blue arm-of-service sign with a white 77. This number was the 11th RHA's unit within the armoured division, identifying them in the order of battle. The red triangle with a white centre signifies that this vehicle belonged to 'A' battery. The WD number is hidden by the crew's packs on the vehicle side armour. This number was preceded by 'S' for self-propelled gun. The vehicle is painted sand and dark earth which has faded and has been covered with dust. Note the large amount of stowage on the vehicle exterior. (IWM).

These Morris Light Reconnaissance cars belonged to a troop of The Royal Air Force Regiment, serving with The First Army. These photographs were taken on the 30th March 1943 and show two cars on patrol. Both cars are finished in dark green. The WD numbers are unreadable on the original prints though their positions can be discerned. R20 is the car number, R21 being the second car in line. The function of the other markings which have been chalked on the lead vehicle are unknown but could be shipping marks. Of particular interest is the personal name and motif painted on car R20. These are shown in the close up of the photograph of the car's Bren Gun turret. The name 'Happy' belongs to the Walt Disney character, in *Snow White and The Seven Dwarfs*, whose face has been expertly painted onto the turret front plate. The metal disc under the name, normally painted bright yellow and containing the bridging class has been overpainted and the troop and vehicle identification painted in. (IWM).

This photograph shows the Squadron Commanders of 56th Battalion Reconnaissance Corps, 78th Infantry Division in their Humber Mark III Light Reconnaissance Cars. Note the variety of finishes on these vehicles. The unit number 41 is white on a horizontally divided square of green upper and blue lower. All cars carry the red, white, red recognition sign on sides and front and are named from the left, Clarion II, Atholl, Faugh-A-Ballagh II and Buaidh-Go-Beace II. Car number 4651984 carries an HQ Squadron diamond and the extreme left car has an 'C' Squadron circle. The other two cars do not sport any visible squadron marks, though it could be assumed that Atholl is A Squadron's Commander's Car and Buaidh-Go-Beace II is B Squadron's. The HQ car does not have the prefix M to its WD number which is present on the other three. All cars have a five-pointed star painted onto their bonnets. (IWM).

RIGHT: Signalman Jack Sheehan on his Aerial Solo Motorcycle. The bike has a WD number painted onto its petrol tank C354652, but of interest is the 2nd New Zealand Division's fern leaf painted on a white background taking up practically all of the front mudguard. (IWM).

BELOW: Two Austin K2/Y Ambulances from the same unit show different styles of markings, as they lead a column of similar types through the Gabes Gap on 6th April 1943. Both vehicles bear the red cross on white backgrounds, the second vehicle having a much larger cross on its side than the lead ambulance. Stretched over both cabs are canvas sheets for aerial recognition, which are different. The lead vehicle has a red cross, whilst the second ambulance bears a roundel which became a common air recognition feature on British vehicles, including tanks. The formation sign on the left front mudguard has (just visible on the original print) the camel of GHQ Middle East, with the unit number 1387 under. There is a formation sign on the right mudguard but this is undecypherable. The lead vehicle has a horseshoe fixed to its radiator grille which is just visible under the muff. Both ambulances carry bridging plates in yellow with bridging classification, a figure 5, painted in. The letter 'C' with the figure 23 below appears on the cab-side of both vehicles. These ambulances are plain sand overall. (IWM).

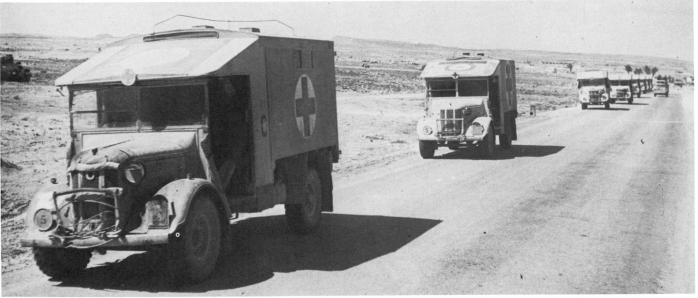

ABOVE: Shermans of the 2nd Lothians and Border Horse, 26th Armoured Brigade, 6th Armoured Division, take part in a victory parade in Tunisia. They are parading past scores of allied troops at the gates of Gambetta Park. The Shermans are finished dark green with the 6th Armoured Divisional badge painted on the bow plate with the unit number in white below.

LEFT: A Sherman of the 9th Lancers with the unit number 86 incorporated with the formation sign of the 1st Armoured Division, moves through the Gabes Gap. The circle on the turret is, or should be, yellow for the 2nd regiment in the brigade. This circle has been block-shaded. A personal name has been painted on the front right dust guard which reads 'Hellzashoot'n' probably taken and modified from the American film comedy 'Hellzapopp'n'. (IWM).

ABOVE: Rhodesian pilots are being driven out to their Hawker Hurricanes in this Chevrolet light truck of The Royal Air Force. Note the standard 'RAF' letters stencilled onto the cab door and the number plate with its Arabic interpretation of the British WD number. The badge on the truck tailgate is the motif found on Rhodesian cap badges. (IWM).

LEFT: A Daimler 'Dingo', two M3 Grants and a Marmon Herrington Armoured Car form part of this 7th Armoured Division Headquarters Group. The Grant is in overall sand camouflage which has worn down to the olive drab original finish especially around the hull door revolver port protectoscope. Carried on the Grant's trackguard is the 7th Armoured Division's badge and the arm-of-service number of 71. The WD number T24224 is painted on the olive drab finish and appears to have been masked over when the Grant received its sand paint. The turret gun has been removed for the command role and replaced by a 37mm gun barrel. Close examination of the original print shows a support bracket holding the barrel to the recuperator housing which is welded in at an acute angle. Removal of the turret gun made room inside for extra map tables and radio equipment. (IWM).

ABOVE: Photographed on the Bou Arada Road in Tunisia, this armoured Crusader Mk III of the 17/21st Lancers (26th Armoured Brigade, 6th Armoured Division) retains its dark green finish. It has a darker colour probably dark earth or black forming a disruptive pattern on the side skirts, where – barely visible under grime – can be seen the red borders of the red, white, red recognition flash. The turret is marked with the circle marking for 'C' squadron, but the teeth of the spare track links are obscuring the troop number inside of this. Other armoured regiments serving in the 26th Armoured Brigade with the 17th/21st Lancers were the 16th/5th Lancers and The 2nd Lothians and Border Horse. Later, these regiments had their tanks replaced by Shermans. (IWM).

RIGHT: The 'Tyne-Tees' badge of the 50th Northumbrian (Infantry) Division is sported by this sand and charcoal camouflaged scout car. The T's on the badge have received a white outline which makes them more prominent from the black background. This 'Dingo' belongs to the divisions Royal Engineer contingent, identified by the blue square under the divisional badge with the figure 70 which is the unit number. The entire motif is painted onto a metal plate. (IWM).

A lorry-load of cheerful-looking German prisoners that were photographed after the attack on Pichon, 8th – 10th April 1943. The lorry is a 3 ton 4 × 2 Bedford OYD of the 6th Armoured Division, the badge of which is clearly displayed on the mudguard: a white armoured fist on a black square. This lorry would probably have been used by the armoured division as a petrol supply vehicle as indicated by the legend 'petrol' on the front bumper. It has a tactical symbol on the cab door which could be interperated as belonging to 'C' Squadron. This tactical sign is repeated over the divisional sign on the mudguard. The lorry has been finished in two-tone camouflage, the demarcation line of which is visible along the bonnet side below the freshly-painted WD number. Note the 6th Armoured Division flash on the uniform of the soldier sitting on the cab roof. (IWM).